Giovanni Aytan

Social Media Marketing in the Self-Media Era

Internet Economics
Internetökonomie

edited by
herausgegeben von

Prof. Dr. Julia Maintz
(Cologne Business School (CBS) –
European University of Applied Sciences)

Volume / Band 12

Giovanni Aytan

Social Media Marketing in the Self-Media Era

A self-experiment on TikTok

This book is printed on acid-free paper.

Bibliographic information published by the Deutsche Nationalbibliothek
The Deutsche Nationalbibliothek lists this publication in the Deutsche Nationalbibliografie; detailed bibliographic data are available in the Internet at http://dnb.dnb.de.

ISBN 978-3-643-91386-9 (pb)
ISBN 978-3-643-96386-4 (PDF)

A catalogue record for this book is available from the British Library.

© LIT VERLAG GmbH & Co. KG Wien,
Zweigniederlassung Zürich 2021
Flössergasse 10
CH-8001 Zürich
Tel. +41 (0) 76-632 84 35
E-Mail: zuerich@lit-verlag.ch   https://www.lit-verlag.ch
Distribution:
In the UK: Global Book Marketing, e-mail: mo@centralbooks.com
In North America: Independent Publishers Group, e-mail: orders@ipgbook.com
In Germany: LIT Verlag Fresnostr. 2, D-48159 Münster
Tel. +49 (0) 2 51-620 32 22, Fax +49 (0) 2 51-922 60 99, e-mail: vertrieb@lit-verlag.de

Preface

In this publication "Social media marketing in the self-media era: A self-experiment on TikTok ", Giovanni Aytan explores the fast-growing social media platform TikTok. TikTok is a key driver of the trend of short video content targeted towards mobile-first young Internet users.

Giovanni Aytan discusses why videos he posted on his channel went viral. At a time, he documents factors influencing the TikTok recommendation algorithm. He moreover analyzes gamification tools and approaches he recommends to use on the platform. Giovanni Aytan thereby compiles good practices for both individual content creators and moreover marketers interested in cutting-edge video marketing.

Julia Maintz
Professor of Internet Economics and International Management
CBS International Business School

Table of Content

Preface V
Table of Figures VIII
1   **Introduction** 1
2   **Social Media Marketing** 3
   2.1 Self-promotion on social media 3
       2.1.1 Social Comparison 4
   2.2 Viral Marketing 5
   2.3 Content Marketing 6
   2.4 Influencer Marketing 7
   2.5 Media Trend: Video Marketing 8
3   **Video Sharing Platform TikTok** 9
   3.1 Teenage girls on TikTok 10
   3.2 TikTok Addiction 11
       3.2.1 Artificial Intelligence 11
       3.2.2 Gamification 12
   3.3 Commercial Models on TikTok 13
   3.4 TikTok Creator Fund 14
4   **Methodology** 16
   4.1 TikTok Experiment 16
   4.2 Mixed Qualitative and Quantitative Approach: Content and Interaction Analysis 18
5   **Discussion: Marketing Strategies on TikTok** 28
   5.1 Cooperating with TikTok Celebrities 28
   5.2 Creating One's Own Channel 29
6   **Conclusion** 31
7   **Study Limitations and Recommendations for Future Research** .. 32
8   **Reference List** 33

Table of Figures

Figure 1:	Statistics about my TikTok account	17
Figure 2:	Statistics about my followers	19
Figure 3:	My first TikTok	20
Figure 4:	My first viral TikTok	21
Figure 5:	Viral video example 2	22
Figure 6:	The hashtag #liebessprüche with over 15.8 million video views	23
Figure 7:	TikTok video about the Corona pandemic	24
Figure 8:	Livestream statistics for October 2020	26
Figure 9:	TikTok Creator Fund overview	27

1 Introduction

This paper discusses the topic of social media marketing on TikTok, a fast-growing social media and video-sharing platform that is extremely popular with teenagers and millennials (INSEAD, 2019). TikTok describes itself as "[…] the leading destination for short-form mobile video" (TikTok, n. d.). Dilon (2020) explains that "with a ray of celebrities quickly adding their profile to the platform, the platform became a source of attraction for teenagers and young adults worldwide" (p. 132). This paper explains why TikTok also becomes increasingly important for marketing purposes – it's likely that a high number of companies and influencers will use it for advertising in the future.

Another important point in this paper involves the media trend of short videos. With the rapid development of the Internet and 4G, short video apps have become very popular (Peng et al., 2019, p. 100) and can be watched almost anywhere. Therefore, it is important to include the topic of video marketing.

Moreover, this paper analyzes the factors of self-media and self-promotion on social media and how they relate to narcissism and social comparison. Self-media has been defined as "independently operated accounts run by individual users posting self-produced content on social media platforms" (IGI Global, n.d.). For instance, users on TikTok produce their own content and also become so-called self-publishing consumers. While people may have always compared themselves to others, this seems especially true now of teenagers, which can motivate and inspire them but can also be detrimental to self-esteem, self-image, and well-being (Newport Academy, 2019). Also, the role of teenage girls on social media will be explained briefly using the most successful TikTok creator Charli D´Amelio. Therefore, this paper discusses the aspect of social comparison on TikTok which is an important point in the self-media era.

The main research question of this paper consists of the topics of social media marketing and self-media, focusing on the video-sharing platform TikTok: How does social media marketing work in the self-media era, taking TikTok as an example?

To answer the research question, it is essential to know how to use TikTok. Therefore, I applied a mix of qualitative and quantitative research, creating my own TikTok account and undertaking a self-experiment to explain how

I used my channel and thus built my own community within about four months. Additionally, this study analyzes several of my viral videos and my channel in detail, based on statistics obtained from the app.

This paper first discusses social media marketing and self-promotion on the Internet and how this leads to social comparison. It explains different forms of social media marketing relevant to TikTok, namely viral marketing, content marketing, influencer marketing, and the media trend of video marketing.

Next, this paper focuses on the video-sharing platform TikTok. It will explain what TikTok actually is and how to use it. After that, this paper will explain the role of teenage girls on TikTok, because they act as role models for many girls. The addiction factors artificial intelligence (AI) and gamification will be expounded. Furthermore, the paper illustrates the different commercial models on this platform.

Subsequently, the self-experiment is explained in detail, along with the realized content and interaction analysis. Based on the research and literature review, two marketing strategies were chosen that can be successfully applied to TikTok.

The conclusion synthesizes the main ideas to answer the research question. Moreover, limitations of this study and recommendations for future research are provided.

2 Social Media Marketing

To answer the main research question about how social media marketing works in the self-media era, using the example of TikTok, we must clarify first what social media marketing is. A definition is given by WordStream, who define social media marketing as "[…] a powerful way for businesses of all sizes to reach prospects and customers" (n.d.). Dilon (2020) mentions that "Social media has increasingly become a major component of our lives" (p. 132). Statista (2020) shows that almost half of humanity uses social media; in January 2020, the number of monthly active users of social networks was around 3.8 billion, which is compared to 2019 an increase of 9.5 percent. According to Saravanakumar and Suganthalakshmi (2012) "[s]ocial media is being widely used by almost all and even the companies, in spite of their size companies have started using social media to advertise and promote themselves" (p. 4445). Social media can help a business or brand in terms of increasing website traffic, building conversions, raising brand awareness, creating brand identity and positive brand association and also improve communication and interaction with their audience (WordStream, n.d.). Therefore, it is important to know how to do social marketing, because "social media can no longer be ignored in the daily agenda of people´s private life and political opinions" (Dilon, 2020, p. 134). This paper focuses on the self-promotion aspect, because many users present themselves on TikTok. Moreover, it analyzes the social comparison aspect, because users tend to compare themselves to others on the platform (for example, their idols on TikTok). Finally, this chapter examines different forms of digital marketing on social media: viral, content, influencer, and video marketing.

2.1 Self-promotion on social media

Social media platforms like Instagram, Facebook, and TikTok provide the opportunity for people to present themselves online. Users can post a picture or video and share it with friends and the world. According to Rui and Stefanone (2013), social media platforms present novel venues for self-disclosure, self-presentation, and impression management (p. 110–118) that were not possible before.

A study by Lee et al. (2015) has shown that Instagram users have five primary social and psychological motives: social interaction, archiving, self-expression, escapism, and peeking (p.552). Another study has also shown that narcissism is one of the most crucial aspects of self-promotional content on social media (Carpenter, 2012, p. 482–486). The term narcissism "refers to a personality trait reflecting a grandiose and inflated self-concept. Specifically, narcissism is associated with positive and inflated self-views" (Buffardi & Campbell, 2008. p. 1304). In addition, individuals who have high levels of narcissism are active on social media platforms (Ong et al., 2001. p. 180–185). These studies suggest that people with narcissistic traits or high levels of narcissism are more likely to post on social media platforms and promote themselves there.

Currently, "internet users are increasingly becoming self-publishing consumers" (Omar & Dequan, 2020, p. 121). TikTok is an example of this. The videos there are mainly based on user-generated content. There is also a limited number of media producers who produce TikTok videos (Omar & Dequan, 2020, p. 122). This has changed the market of video-sharing platforms (discussed later) and has led to a self-media era in which the users become producers.

According to Kumar and Prabha (2019), TikTok allows users to act like celebrities for a few minutes, especially if their video goes viral, and this creates an illusion whereby an anonymous person is considered an internet star (p. 76). Moreover, the "wide reach of the videos via social media platforms gives them instant gratification because of this boosting up of 'self-identity'" (Kumar & Prabha, 2019, p. 76). The self is in the foreground and is an important aspect of social media. In this era of self-media, people try to promote themselves, and TikTok supports this.

2.1.1 Social Comparison

As stated, social comparison has increased in the self-media era. According to Wood (1996), "social comparison is defined as the process of thinking about information about one or more other people in relation to the self" (p. 520–521).

Social media reinforces the negative impact of social comparison on teens because they compare themselves to celebrities or others who have achieved at unusually high levels, and as a result, many teens feel that their own accomplishments are not enough (Newport Academy, 2019).

Research has also shown that TikTok users try to imitate other users who are perceived to be similar to themselves to boost their self-esteem (Kumar

& Prabha, 2019, p. 76). Kumar and Prabha (2019) have added that due to the virtual competition to get more likes, some videos are glamorous with the intention of gaining more viewers (p. 76). In these ways, some people do not reveal their real personas on social media and try to be another person or a better version of themselves. For example, Barry et al. (2017) have stated that insecure women are more likely to post sexualized photographs to construct themselves as desirable (p. 48–60).

Studies have also shown that this comparison to other people on image-focused apps can lead to mental issues like body dissatisfaction, eating disorders, and narcissistic personalities (Jaffar et al., 2019, p. 187). The reason is that people compare themselves to the positive posts of others and feel that those people have better lives (Chou & Edge, 2012, p. 117–118). Similarly, Lup et al. (2015) have found that people who follow more strangers on Instagram are more likely to have symptoms of depression than those who follow fewer strangers (p. 247–252). This shows a high level of self-comparison to others, which may lead to the point that people find themselves less attractive.

As can be seen, social comparison can lead to many problems in society, and TikTok is a platform that corresponds to the current era of self-media. In comparison to Instagram, the social comparison aspect on TikTok is not as strong as on Instagram. This will be explained in the chapter teenage girls on TikTok. TikTok probably enhances social comparison and must be further observed in future research regarding negative consequences on people.

2.2 Viral Marketing

In order to answer the main research question of this paper, viral marketing must be considered, as TikTok encourages going viral and reaching as many people as possible. Viral marketing "describes any strategy that encourages individuals to pass on a marketing message to others, creating the potential for exponential growth in the message´s exposure and influence" (Wilson, 2000). It is also known as word of mouth (WOM) or buzz marketing applied to social media (Miller & Lammas, 2010, p. 3).

Wilson (2000) has compared viral marketing contents to a virus because they show rapid reception growth and can reach thousands to millions of people very quickly. Helm (2000) has further argued that compared to traditional WOM communication, the internet is more effective because it is easier and faster to reach more people around the world (p. 158–161).

It has also been suggested that a benefit of viral marketing is that it is relatively inexpensive compared to other marketing methods. On the other hand, it holds risks for marketers because they do not have control over the spread of the message, which can lead to a potential negative impact from a viral campaign (Woerndl et al., 2008, p. 36). For example, if a message is misinterpreted, it can damage the brand image. Therefore, marketers must think carefully about their campaign.

Woerndl (2008) has also stated that messages that foster imagination and provide entertainment are more likely to be voluntarily shared by others (p. 37). Therefore, a viral marketing campaign should be interactive.

As suggested from these studies, TikTok would be a suitable platform for viral marketing. The self-experiment in this study shows in detail how I managed to go viral.

2.3 Content Marketing

Another type of digital marketing is content marketing. According to the Content Marketing Institute, this is "a strategic marketing approach focused on creating and distributing valuable, relevant, and consistent content to attract and retain a clearly defined audience and, ultimately, to drive profitable customer action" (2015). The content can be in the form of a video, an image, a text, and so forth.

Due to the importance of the internet, digital content marketing is an online marketing strategy preferred by many companies (Vinerean, 2017, p. 94). Vinerean (2017) has also stated that brands and companies can share their brand stories on various social media platforms like Facebook, Twitter, or Instagram (p. 94). TikTok would be a relatively new platform on which to do so.

As discussed, viral marketing is an effective strategy. Therefore, marketers try to combine it with content marketing. Studies have shown that users should create positive content with useful information, and people will share it to help others (Berger & Milkman, 2012, p. 192). Berger and Milkman (2012) have added that negative content is not shared as much as positive content (p. 192).

As this paper focuses on the video-sharing platform TikTok, video content is the most important factor. Such content can be highly engaging and is easily sharable via social media (McGill, 2017). Although videos require a larger investment of time and resources than written content, they are shared 40 times more often than other types of content, and they also get people's attention more easily than other content formats (McGill, 2017). Therefore, TikTok is an appropriate platform for content marketing because it is geared toward short videos that attract people's attention.

2.4 Influencer Marketing

People, especially younger generations, spend hours watching YouTube videos in which their favorite influencers are playing games, reviewing products, or just posting about their daily activities (Veirman et al., 2019). The popularity of such content on social media platforms like YouTube and TikTok has inspired advertisers to invest in the growing market of influencer marketing (Lou, 2020).

Influencer marketing has been defined as "a rapidly growing industry that attempts to promote products or increase brand awareness through content spread by social media users who are considered to be influential" (Carter, 2016, p. 2). Generally, these influencers have a large number of social media followers and are assumed to be trusted voices that can reach a large audience (Carter, 2016, p. 2). In exchange, the influencers receive free products or are paid for a mention in their videos or for creating a sponsored video (Veirman et al., 2019). An example of such advertising would be getting an influencer on YouTube to play a mobile game and review it. In addition, firms also include promo codes that can be used by followers for a discount at the checkout; in this way, marketers can determine the success of their influencer marketing strategy (GRIN, n.d.).

Statista (2018), an online platform for statistics, forecasted the market volume of influencer marketing in the DACH region (Germany, Austria, and Switzerland) for 2020. They included all monetary and non-monetary income of German-speaking influencers with at least 10,000 followers in Germany, Austria, and Switzerland. In 2017, the market was about 560 million Euro. For 2020, they estimated a revenue of approximately 990 million Euro. This shows that this market is becoming popular and will probably keep growing in the future. Therefore, marketers should consider using this marketing strategy to be successful.

2.5 Media Trend: Video Marketing

To fully answer the research question, the media trend of short videos and platforms on which to share them (such as TikTok) must be considered as they are becoming more popular. According to Qiyang and Jung (2019), short-video platforms are mainly used on mobile applications, where users can create, edit, share, and view short videos. The videos have a standardized duration ranging from seconds to a few minutes (p. 2).

Yang et al. (2019) have posited that the rise of mobile internet technology allowed a variety of short-video software, which created a short-video era for the audience and gave videos new connotations and importance (p. 340). Among them, the short-video-sharing platform TikTok is currently trending.

Cheng et al. (2013) have stated that YouTube, which was established in 2005, has become the most successful internet website, providing a new generation of short-video-sharing services (p. 1184). Cheng et al. (2013) have also stated that YouTube alone consumed as much bandwidth as the entire internet did in the year 2000 (p. 1184). Holland (2016) has further explained that since Google bought YouTube, it went from a platform where amateur and ad-free videos were posted to one that concentrates on the consumer through commercialization and professional videos (p. 1). Thus, YouTube helped to make short videos popular and created job opportunities for many people. This same process can also be witnessed regarding the short-video-sharing platform TikTok.

Researchers have argued the existence of information overload; people's attention is a scarce resource, and whoever captures it has the potential to retain users and gain wealth (Hu, 2020, p. 59). Therefore, an important factor on TikTok is that the videos should quickly grab the user´s attention. Furthermore, the more relevant, creative, and entertaining a video is, the more valuable it will be to the user, thus catching their attention. These are all important points for the video-sharing platform TikTok. In the next chapter, TikTok will be introduced in more detail.

3   Video Sharing Platform TikTok

For this paper, an understanding of what TikTok is and how it became so popular is essential. Therefore, this chapter presents a definition of the video platform and what can be done there. After that, it discusses the aspects of AI and gamification on TikTok, which make it addictive to users. It then analyzes the commercial models on TikTok and how they support creators with the so-called TikTok Creator Fund.

First, TikTok has been described as "a social media platform targeted at young, mobile-first users" (Guinaudeau et al., 2020, p. 3). According to Statista (2020), TikTok has over 800 million users worldwide, and 69% of active users are between 16 and 24 years old (FUTURE BIZ, 2020), which shows that the target group of this app consists of younger people—more precisely, Generation Z.

At its beginning, the app was called musical.ly and had over 100 million users, but in August 2018, it was taken over by a Chinese company called Byte Dance, and its users, with all of their content and accounts, were moved to TikTok (Influencer Marketing Hub, n.d.).

On this platform, users can find videos from all fields such as comedy, cooking, drawing, singing, or dancing. All content is user generated. Guinaudeau et al. (2020) have shown that the app offers an extremely wide range for customizing these videos, for example, with emojis and other text superimposed on the video, filters, or video effects (p. 3). The length of a TikTok clip is a maximum of 60 seconds; research has shown that "the short video within one minute is the best advertisement for a product" (Gong, 2019, p. 374). Thus, the platform is a good foundation for advertising.

For a video, producers can choose a sound, which can be a song excerpt, music or a sound effect from the TikTok sound gallery. There is also the option to create own sounds (the topic of sounds is discussed in detail in the practical part of this paper). Moreover, video makers can participate in trending challenges, react to other videos, or lip sync.

However, what sets this platform apart from other social media platforms is the "for you" page. The goal of TikTok creators is to land on this page to get the widest range of viewers possible and go viral. Even if users do not follow a specific person, they will see their videos on this page when they open the app and land directly on it. In addition, this page does not have a specified end. On TikTok, every video is on someone's "for you" page, and when the algorithm determines that many people like a video, it will be shown more often on the "for you" pages of other people. In this way, "TikTok tries to [...] guarantee an audience for every post" (Guinaudeau et al. 2020, p 9).

Thus, Tolentino (2019) has described TikTok as the social network that has nothing to do with the user´s own social network because the number of followers is not as important as the quality of the videos. This is the biggest difference between TikTok and all other existing social media platforms.

The biggest influencer on TikTok is Charli D´Amelio with over 100 million followers. In the next chapter, her success will be analyzed.

3.1 Teenage girls on TikTok

Teenage girls on TikTok is a very important topic, because Kennedy states that "[...] the most-followed stars of TikTok are not only young, but female, normatively feminine, white and wealthy" (2020, p. 1071). For young teens, TikTok is a place "[...] to be silly, unashamed, unfiltered – a tonic to the earnestness of Instagram, the stress of Snapchat, the verbal warfare of Twitter" (Lamont, 2020). The reason for this is, that many young girls simply make their videos in their bedrooms, where you can see clothes, make-up or even shoes in the background (Kennedy, 2020, p. 2072). Lamont explains that "TikTok´s strategy of appealing to Gen Z´s need for release, somewhere for them to not be Insta-perfect, was working" (2020). The Sunday Times (2020) reinforces this message, because they present Instagram as glossy and filtered, while TikTok would be goofy and relatable. From this, it can be concluded, that TikTok is a fun place for young teenagers, where they can feel comfortable. The fun aspect will also play an important role in the gamification chapter, which will be discussed later on.

The most successful TikTok creator is the young teenage girl Charli D´Amelio.

According to Kennedy (2020), on 25 March 2020 global news providers announced that the 15-year-old American teenager Charli D´Amelio had become the most followed person on TikTok (p. 1070). Currently, she has over 100 million followers (as of December 2020). Her videos are just a few seconds long. Most of the time she is dancing, or she is doing lip-sync videos in her room. She also always creates her own versions of a dance, which other people imitate then. Charli D´Amelio character on TikTok fits perfectly to TikTok´s image. In her videos, she is laughing, winking, sticking out her tongue, with her screwed up eyes to signal happiness and carefree aesthetics. She also shows videos where she makes mistakes in a dance choreography, or she posts videos with her family (Kennedy, 2020, p. 1072). Kennedy (2020) also shows that her style of clothing, mostly hoodies, hot pants and joggers are normal and relatable, and that she indicates her viewers that she is still feminine and sexually desirable (p. 1071). It can be concluded that Charli D´Amelio wants to show that she is a completely normal person like all other people. According to Bennet, Charli D'Amelio´s long time bio was "I don't get the hype either" (2020). This confirms the statement that she feels like a completely normal American teenage girl. She exudes a perfectly normal lifestyle. Millions of other teenage girls take her as a role model, which then leads to social comparison. How strong social comparison is on TikTok is not decisive for this paper, but can be included in future research to analyze TikTok´s influence on people, especially on teens. In the next chapter this paper will show why TikTok is so addictive and why people use this app.

3.2 TikTok Addiction

Thus far, this paper has clarified what TikTok is, including information about its algorithm. However, to answer the research question about how social media marketing works in the self-media era, we must know more about the reasons why TikTok is so addictive. That requires an analysis of the AI and gamification tools on this platform.

3.2.1 Artificial Intelligence

Artificial intelligence "refers to the simulation of human intelligence in machines that are programmed to think like humans and mimic their actions. The term may also be applied to any machine that exhibits traits associated with the human mind such as learning and problem-solving" (Frankenfield, 2020). Basically, AI tries to imitate the human brain.

According to INSEAD Knowledge (2019, p. 1), TikTok relies on AI in two ways. The first involves the consumer side because the algorithm quickly learns what consumers want to see based on how long they actually watch a video or if they like or comment on a video. The short clips easily create a sizable dataset that the AI can use to determine videos the consumer wants to see. Secondly, AI also helps producers create viral videos with the use of filters, hashtags, or suggested music.

INSEAD Knowledge (2019, p. 1) has explained that the average time spent on TikTok is 52 minutes per day, and in this timeframe, a consumer may watch over 200 videos. This data feeds the algorithm every day, and its learning improves. Because of this well-working algorithm—which sometimes knows more than consumers what they want to see—TikTok entices users to stay in the app. However, future research on the TikTok algorithm will be needed, as the algorithm is continuously being improved.

3.2.2 Gamification

Another addictive factor is gamification. According to Salen and Zimmermann (2003), a game is a system in which players engage in an artificial conflict, defined by rules that result in a quantifiable outcome (p. 96). Hromek and Roffey (2009) argue that the element of fun is paramount for a young person playing a game (p. 630). Thus, social media platforms try to use game elements to make using the respective platform fun and joyful; this is called gamification.

"[G]amification refers to a process of enhancing a service with affordances for gameful experiences in order to support users' overall value creation" (Huatori & Hamari, 2017, p. 25). TikTok does exactly that. With different game elements, it attempts to create a playful experience on the platform.

Lucassen and Jansen (2014) have further clarified that gamifying an experience (in this case, TikTok) raises the time a user spends on the platform (p. 197). According to Lusch and Vargo (2004), the users are the value creators of a platform, so TikTok (which is user generated) ensures that it enhances interaction (p. 240–242) with gamification elements. Game-like functions include participating in livestreams and liking, sharing, or commenting on posts. In addition, the TikTok livestreams also have gamification elements. For example, users can buy TikTok currency and donate it to other users in their livestreams, and participants see an animation appear. People who want their name to appear with a gamified animation will then also buy in-app currency and donate it.

Rewards are also an important element of gamification on social media; according to Miller et. al. (2013), rewards increase participation in and the motivation to do a specific task (p. 9–16). TikTok's rewards for content creators mean that their videos are going viral, they can earn money from it (this aspect is discussed later in the self-experiment), or they are rewarded with likes, comments, and shares.

The conclusion from this is that a gamified online environment is a crucial aspect of a social media platform and should not be neglected. The use of gamification elements increases users' addiction to the platform and leads to a more playful environment. Therefore, it is important for an app like TikTok to utilize it.

Gamification and AI are the two main reasons why TikTok is considered to be so addictive. Nonetheless, TikTok must continue work so that it does not become boring and monotonous for users. Future research and studies about the use of gamification elements on TikTok could enhance its performance.

3.3 Commercial Models on TikTok

There are three core commercials models on TikTok: advertising, e-commerce, and livestreaming. The following paragraphs refer to Yingjia Hu´s (2020) recent research about TikTok (p. 61–63), starting with advertising, which is still the main source of money for many video-sharing platforms. The main advertising models on TikTok are open-screen ads, infomercials, product placements, custom challenges, and sticker partnerships (Hu, 2020, p. 61).

On TikTok, open-screen ads appear directly after a user opens the app. They are usually five-second videos or pictures. Hu (2020) explains that on TikTok brands can use this efficiently for brand exposure because it reaches users directly and reduces the intermediate link (p. 61).

However, infomercials are the main advertising model on TikTok. These are basically ads used in the content feed that viewers can also see on other social media platforms like Instagram, where they can find sponsored posts among the content they are watching. In addition, these ads can be targeted to a specific group that will probably like the ad; if not, it can be easily ignored.

The next advertising model is product placement. These are ads in which people show a brand's products in their video.

Sticker ads are also a popular form of advertisement on TikTok. These are "the brand message included in the built-in video" (Hu, 2020, p. 61).

The last form of advertisement consists of customized challenges. These are quite exclusive because they cannot be found on other social media platforms (Hu, 2020, p. 61). With this marketing method, brands create challenges in which users and influencers can participate, in order to increase their reach.

The second core commercial model after advertising is e-commerce. In this case, the social media influencer cooperates with e-commerce companies that match with their content, or they can even create their own e-commerce company. For example, a user can create merchandise, e.g. clothes, and wear them in TikTok videos - or place a link to the own shop in the user profile.

The last core commercial model is livestreaming. According to Johnson and Woodcock (2019), "[l]ivestreaming has emerged in recent years as a major new topic in media and communication studies" (p. 2). Hu (2020) has mentioned that through livestreaming, one can interact with fans in real time. For example, the popular and successful streaming platform Twitch uses the monetization strategy of donations, whereby users give money to a streamer and get recognition in exchange (Anderson, 2017, p. 1–16). TikTok has also implemented the donation function in which users can buy in-game currency and donate it to streamers. As mentioned, TikTok even uses gamification elements here because different animations appear depending on how much one has donated.

But other platforms are still better in livestreaming. On TikTok, it is mainly based on the need for interaction between fans and users (p. 62). For example, TikTok should allow livestreaming via PC or have subscription functions like the other streaming platforms.

These core commercial models, along with exclusive elements like custom challenges, create a unique selling point, although the livestreams should be improved for TikTok to compete with other platforms like Twitch or YouTube.

3.4 TikTok Creator Fund

The TikTok Creator Fund is a fund from TikTok which helps to support the creators on the platform. To be a part of the TikTok Creator Fund, users must be older than 18, have at least 10,000 followers, and have received over 10,000 video views in the last 30 days (TikTok, 2020). If a user meets all the criteria, he can apply for it in the app. In Europe, it was launched in 2020 with approximately $70 million, but the fund is expected to rise to $300 million within three years and will be extended to more markets in Europe (TikTok, 2020). In the United States, this fund is expected to grow to over $1 billion in the next three years (TikTok, 2020).

TikTok tries to support and encourage users to make creative content: "We hope this fund will continue to support our creator community through rewarding innovative and creative content" (TikTok, 2020). Vanessa Pappas (2020), the general manager of TikTok US, said: "Through the TikTok Creator Fund, our creators will be able to realize additional earnings that help reward the care and dedication they put into creatively connecting with an audience that's inspired by their ideas." This is intended to show that TikTok cares about its users and the quality of content on the platform. In addition, users must follow the community guidelines or be removed from the funding program.

The next parts of this paper are dedicated to my own TikTok account and its performance.

4 Methodology

To determine how social media marketing works in the self-media era, this paper uses a mixed qualitative and quantitative approach. I created my own TikTok account as a case study in an attempt to create my own community there. The goal of this project was to create a base of at least 10,000 followers. I started this self-experiment on August 11th, 2020. This paper analyzes the values until November 28th, 2020, to show what is possible on TikTok in this time period when one starts from zero.

For this experiment, I tried to post every day to generate as many followers and likes as possible. This paper analyzes several of my successful TikTok videos and shows the quantitative data (for example, statistics such as video views in the last 28 days, profile views, etc.). In addition, screenshots are used to demonstrate details.

The results of this self-experiment are intended to help future researchers as well as brands and users who want to create their own TikTok channels.

This experiment increased my knowledge about the TikTok algorithm and how companies should collaborate with influencers on this platform. Moreover, it shows that influencers and firms that are not active on this platform should use it to grow a community quickly and easily compared to other social media and video-sharing platforms.

4.1 TikTok Experiment

This section provides an overview of my TikTok channel and content. The name of the channel is YoungGoku47 (see Figure 1); Goku is a character in the famous anime "Dragon Ball," and most of the time, especially at the beginning of my TikTok career, I wore an orange shirt from this anime. 47 is my favorite number and does not have a specific meaning.

The content on my TikTok channel mostly consists of jokes and love sayings. I try to use sounds that are trending, but I also create my own (discussed further in the content and interaction analysis). I mostly tried to be creative and invented the jokes and sayings myself. However, sometimes for inspiration, I looked at, for example, what American creators did, which helped me to create more content. I don't speak in any video, but there are some exceptions where you can hear my voice, because I try to integrate my personality more into the videos.

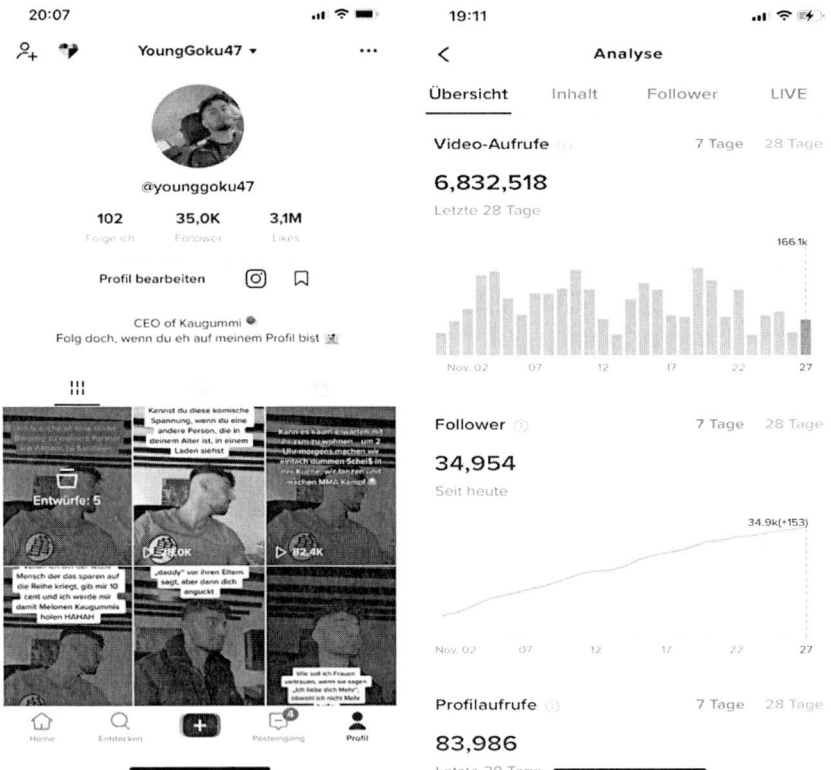

Figure 1: Statistics about my TikTok account
Note: Screenshots taken from my TikTok account, YoungGoku47

Because I wore this orange shirt in the beginning of my TikTok career and always chewed gum in my videos, people recognized me, and these two things became my trademarks. I slightly changed this later so it would not become too monotonous.

Most of the time, I posted one to four videos a day. I only wanted quality content, so I deleted those that did not reach over 10,000 views after one day. Others can argue whether or not that was right, but for my channel and this experiment, I only wanted videos that were well received. Generally, I received 30,000 to 200,000 views per video. Compared to other TikTok users, and considering my follower base of 35,000, this is a very strong and uncommon result.

During this self-experiment, I tested the livestreaming function and interacted with my community. I also received several donations, which did not amount to much (as shown later in the paper).

4.2 Mixed Qualitative and Quantitative Approach: Content and Interaction Analysis

For this paper, I decided to have a mixed qualitative and quantitative approach. The qualitative aspect would be my videos and the quantitative aspect would be the statistics of the videos. Therefore, this section analyzes the content of my channel and shows the statistics relating to several videos, as well as some examples.

On November 28th, 2020, I had 34,954 followers and over three million likes on all of my videos. Figure 1 shows the past video views of the last 28 days, which were around 6.8 million. I can see exactly how many video views I have per day. The statistics show that this fluctuates daily because not every video goes viral. Under video views, a graph shows how many followers I generate per day (currently around 200 daily). This also depends whether a video goes viral, because then the number increases. In addition, the bottom of the profile reveals the calls of the past 28 days (around 84,000); this indicates when people who see one of my videos on their "for you" page go to my profile to watch more of my content.

Figure 2 depicts statistics and information about my followers, around 70% of whom are female. This indicates that I should generate more content related to female TikTok users, because they are the main target group of my channel. This is a very important information for me and helps me to create videos.

In addition, figure 2 shows that my main target group is from Germany, and a small part is from the other German-speaking countries Austria and Switzerland. It also shows the time at which my followers are active. As seen in the graph, on November 27th, 2020, follower activity was constant from 2:00 p.m. because this was a Saturday, when many users are home and have time for TikTok. Most viewers (14,000) were active at 9:00 p.m., which is an important statistic to determine the optimum time to post a video. If more people are watching it directly, the video is more likely to go viral. For example, it would not make sense to post early in the morning; for that day, I would post in the evening around six.

Mixed Qualitative and Quantitative Approach

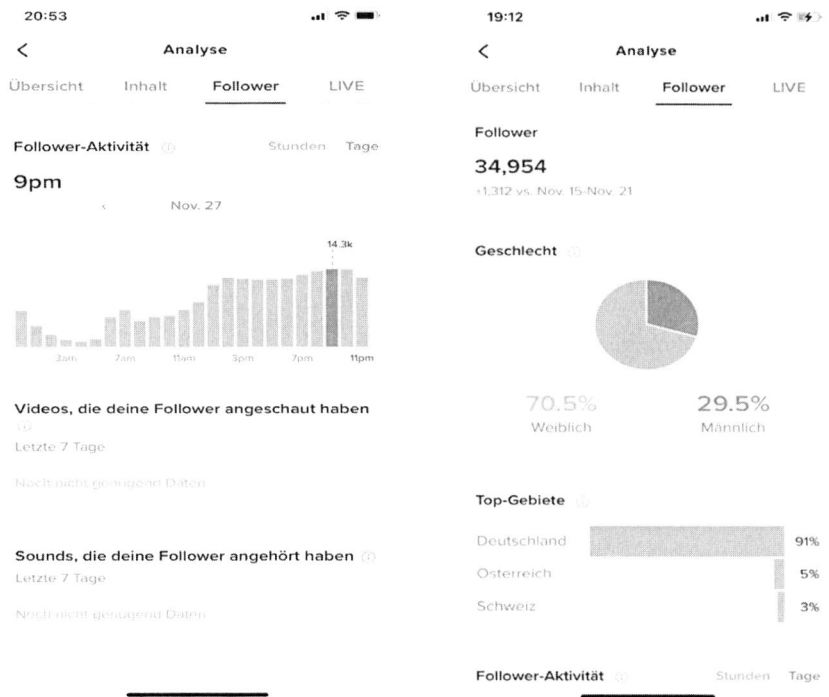

Figure 2: Statistics about my followers
   Note: Statistics taken from my TikTok account

In the past, TikTok also included other follower statistics under follower activity (for example, videos or sounds that a follower recently watched or listened to). These statistics could help creators know more about what their followers want to see. However, they are currently not working, and TikTok has made no official statement about it.

At the beginning of my TikTok career, I was not sure what to post. Therefore, I decided to post a random video in which I played with bey blades. This is a toy for kids, and I wanted to see how it would perform. (The statistics can be found in Figure 3.) As the results show, this first video had 604 views, 27 likes, eight comments, and one share. The average playback time was 10 seconds, but the video was 12.19 seconds long (as described later, this is a crucial factor on TikTok). It can also be seen that 81% of the traffic came from the "for you" page, while 17% was from my profile (people who watched my later posts and came to my profile to see other videos).

Figure 3: My first TikTok
  Note: Statistics about my first video taken from my TikTok account

This video can no longer be seen on my TikTok channel because it does not fit the content I do now. Therefore, I deleted it. However, this video exemplifies that creators do not need followers on TikTok to reach an audience. With zero followers, I managed to get over 600 views. This is a unique selling point that sets TikTok apart from all other platforms. The algorithm enables an easy start where every video has the prerequisites to go viral.

In the next few days, I posted different kinds of videos. I tried to be creative and find something what the people really want to see. After just a few days, I had a breakthrough on August 13th, 2020, with a video that went viral (see Figure 4). In this video, I was wearing the orange shirt from the series "Dragon Ball" and just looked out the window with my back to the camera. I used a trending sound at that time which was the Star Wars melody. I also wrote a joke that fit the video and sound. The translation for the joke would be the following: "I just realized that guys put their headsets on for the same reason that girls put their makeup on. To play with the boys." Due to the success of this video, I continued doing jokes and creating content that would fit my target group. People also loved my orange "Dragon Ball" shirt, and soon it became one of my trademarks.

As seen in Figure 4, that video has over 130,000 views and more than 10,000 likes. I gained more followers, and there were days when I generated 1,000 per day. This has slowed due to increased competition (explained later).

Figure 4: My first viral TikTok
 Note: Statistics about my first viral video taken from my TikTok account

Figure 5 shows another of my successful videos. It was posted on September 17th, 2020 and got over 700,000 views and more than 130,000 likes. This TikTok video is in third place regarding a sound that was trending at that time. Therefore, if a user clicks on the sound, my video is shown at the top. I also used the colored filter effect which is like a disco filter with different LED lights; this also became one of my trademarks because I use it in most of my videos. In just sat in my chair and looked up sadly. The translation for the quote in Figure 5 would be: "Actors kiss and don't fall in love for seven years, but when someone opens the door for me, I think about it for six months."

Figure 5: Viral video example 2
  Note: Taken from my TikTok channel and from the sound gallery (link to the TikTok: https://vm.tiktok.com/ZSgCLP2c/)

In addition, I used the hashtags #crush, #love, and #lovesayings, though hashtags do not often play a big role in a video going viral (in quite a few of my videos with many views and likes, I did not even use one hashtag). Other popular TikTok creators never use hashtags. For instance "mcamiri"

Mixed Qualitative and Quantitative Approach

is a female TikTok user who mostly posts dance videos and never uses any hashtags, nevertheless she has over 480,000 followers and more than 55 million likes on all of her videos.

It can be concluded from my self-experiment that if a creator uses a specific hashtag, they can get additional views, but it is not a major factor for going viral on TikTok. (Figure 6 shows that many of my videos are under the hashtag #liebessprüche, which results in a small number of additional views, though they remain constant.) A more important factor is being among the first to use trending sounds, which results in more video views. When sounds are trending, this leads to more direct views, but if the sound is not trending anymore, the videos are barely watched.

Figure 6: The hashtag #liebessprüche with over 15.8 million video views
 Note: Screenshot taken from the TikTok search for the hashtag #liebessprüche

24   Methodology

For my most popular TikTok post (see Figure 7), I made a joke about how the German government addressed the Corona pandemic in schools. (They decided that the windows must be open in class, though many people argued that the government should close the schools instead to reduce infections. This is a controversial topic, which is why this video went viral.) The translation for the quote in Figure 7 would be: Today I was in the hospital and opened the windows of the Corona patients, suddenly everyone was cured. I also used the colored filter effect again and smiled with my thumbs up to the right.

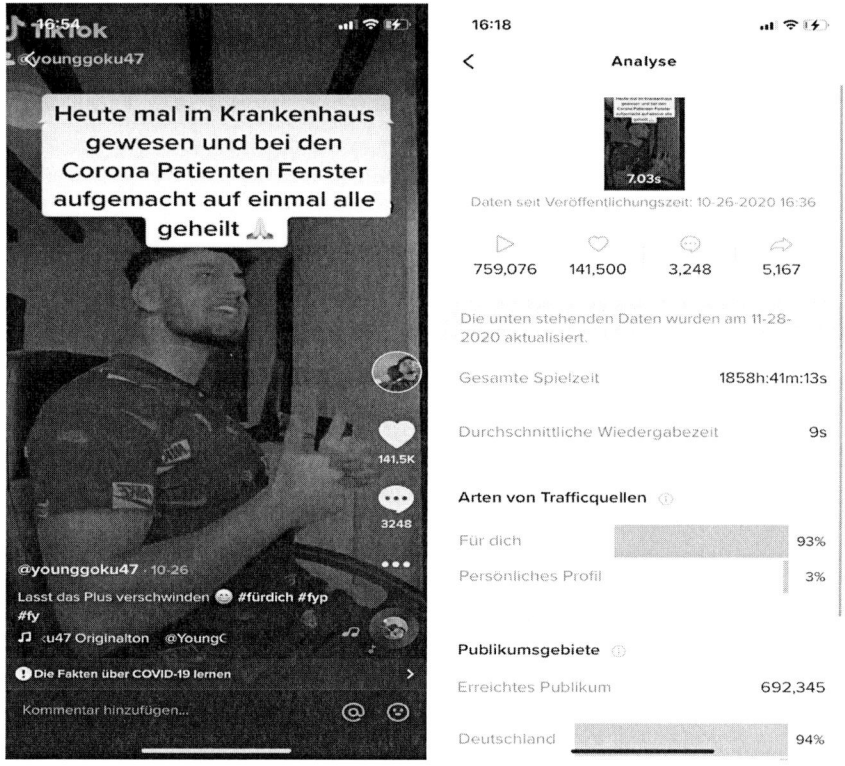

Figure 7: TikTok video about the Corona pandemic
          Note: Screenshots taken from my TikTok channel (link to the video: https://vm.tiktok.com/ZSgGEM5B/)

As seen in Figure 7, the video has over 750,000 views, over 140,000 likes, over 3,200 comments, and over 5,000 shares. It is exactly 7.03 seconds long, while the average watch time is nine seconds. This means that many people watched the video more than once. I realized that the watch time is a crucial factor for the TikTok algorithm. If the average watch time is much longer than the video, there is a high probability that the video will go viral. Another crucial factor for the algorithm is the share function. The more shares a video has, the more likely it is to go viral because TikTok wants to get more people on the app. Therefore, it is always god to create content which people like to share (viral marketing).

Moreover, many people made controversial videos about the pandemic, and TikTok reacted by putting a little banner under every post about COVID-19 (seen in Figure 7 on the bottom). The algorithm automatically detects posts about the pandemic, and when users press on the banner, they land on the TikTok channel of the World Health Organization, where there is information related to the Corona pandemic. This helps people to learn more about COVID-19 and stops the spread of so-called fake news.

Additionally, I created my own sound, "Originalton—younggoku47," and used it in this video (as seen in Figure 7). To make this sound, I used a song from Akon and changed the speed of his singing. By pressing on the sound, it can be seen that there are a total of 49 videos (as of December 15th, 2020) with that sample. Thus, it is also possible to create a trending sound, which brings more attention to one's videos. However, I usually used already trending sounds because creating audio was not the focus of the experiment.

For the experiment, I also did several livestreams and interacted with my community. I mostly talked about myself and showed my community more of my character. For example, I answered a lot of questions about my hobbies or what I did today. In addition, every time I didn't chew gum on my streams, I got approached, because that's a trademark of mine. Figure 8 shows my statistics for October 2020: 14 livestreams with a total of 11,200 views and a length of around nine hours. As seen in the figure, I gained 36 followers only through streaming and received donations of 311 diamonds, which is about $1.50. TikTok tries to encourage livestreams, so several people land on other people's "for you" page. In addition, the platform recently developed a tab for livestreams, where users can browse through different streams. Moreover, TikTok added a function which allows you to invite randomly selected users with at least 1000 followers who are currently streaming. The other users are always from abroad and the only way to stream with users who speak the same language is if you follow each other. Then, when both are streaming, you can send each other a request. It's a great way to get to know other users and to entertain your community.

Figure 8: Livestream statistics for October 2020
Note: Statistics taken from my TikTok account

In addition to donations, I also received money from the TikTok Creator Fund which I applied for on September 19th, 2020, when I reached 10,000 followers. Figure 9 shows that I earned 303.37 euros between then and November 25th, 2020. Dividing that sum by the period (67 days) amounts to approximately 4.5 euros per day, though Figure 9 depicts that the amount changes on a daily basis. For example, on November 23th, I gained only 1.62 euros, while I received 7.99 euros on November 19th. This is because

Mixed Qualitative and Quantitative Approach 27

not all of my videos went viral. However, the amount of money that a creator gets per view is not exactly known because there is no official statement from TikTok.

While it would not be possible to live independently from the Creator Fund alone, it helps many people, for example, to buy equipment for their videos. It is also a motivation to create good content and continue to post videos.

Figure 9: TikTok Creator Fund overview
  Note: Screenshot taken from my TikTok account

Based on the results of this experiment, it is possible to generalize success factors for an inclusion in marketing strategies for TikTok, which will be discussed in the next chapter.

5 Discussion: Marketing Strategies on TikTok

The experiment was a success because the goal was to get 10,000 followers, and I currently have over 30,000. However, the growth is not as strong as it previously was due to increased competition. For instance, if a user posts a creative idea on TikTok, many people will copy it or be inspired by it (many people are now posting videos with quotes and jokes like mine). What sets me apart from them are my trademarks, my humor and my way of creating videos. But to stay relevant on TikTok, regular videos are mandatory.

Additionally, the number of TikTok users is increasing steadily; according to Statista (2020), in October 2020, the app was downloaded from the Apple app store around 200,000 times in Germany alone. These are all factors that increase the competition.

For the experiment, I sometimes created videos that did not fit my usual content, and they received very few views. Therefore, a successful strategy is for creators to post videos that match their content and character on TikTok. In addition, they can also create their own version of a trend. For example, I used trending sounds, but produced distinct videos to stay special and get noticed. The same works for brands, which should have creative and original content to distinguish themselves from the competition.

Nevertheless, not many companies or brands are currently using TikTok. Therefore, the business competition is not that strong, so this platform can be used to promote products and services. Instead of using traditional forms of advertising, brands should follow the trends of user-generated content, influencer marketing, viral marketing, short videos, and the self-promotion aspect of social media.

However, each brand must determine which marketing strategy to follow on TikTok. Thus, the following sections discuss two forms of marketing on this platform: cooperating with TikTok celebrities and creating one's own account.

5.1 Cooperating with TikTok Celebrities

As the TikTok algorithm shows users content based on what they like, it is easy for brands to cooperate with creators. For example, a beauty brand could promote its products via a beauty celebrity on TikTok. This would be an easy form of influencer marketing and product placement, whereby a web celebrity releases a video about brand products on his or her channel.

Figure 10 illustrates what it looks like when a company works together with a TikTok user. Here, Amazon Prime partnered with the influencer Paulomac who has over 800,000 followers on TikTok and is famous for funny sketches. In this video, he is doing a comedy sketch about Amazon Prime and how beneficial it is for students. The idea is basically that Paulomac posts the same content he usually does but for Amazon Prime. Viewers will recognize him and probably watch the whole video. However, this video cannot be found on the Amazon Prime channel because it is purely an advertisement which links directly to the registration page of Amazon Prime.

This marketing strategy works well on TikTok. By using a short video combined with influencer marketing, this advertisement for Amazon Prime received over 100,000 likes.

5.2 Creating One's Own Channel

Another strategy is for a brand to create its own TikTok channel. My self-experiment shows that this method can work quickly if a company has creative ideas. The strategy used in my experiment can serve as a general guide: Find what works on this platform. Create one's own sounds. Start one's own challenges and partake in current challenges. Be creative to stand out from the crowd and the competition.

An example of this marketing strategy is the brand 4bro, a company promoting lifestyle products, especially food and drinks. It started to launch its products in April 2020, during the first lockdown (Startup Valley, 2020). In an interview with Startup Valley (2020), the founder, Engin Ergün, has explained that the target group is between 15 and 35, which is relatively young and fits TikTok's demographics. Therefore, the company created a TikTok channel, and since the launch in April, it amassed over 80,000 followers. The brand posts creative videos that suit the lifestyle it represents. Additionally, the company participates in challenges and creates its own. Furthermore, 4bro works with other TikTok creators and posts these videos on its channel, but the company also sends packages to other influencers who fit the lifestyle depicted by the brand. This strategy has resulted in nearly all German TikTok users being familiar with the brand.

In summary, these two marketing strategies work well on TikTok. In an era of self-media, when consumers are becoming self-publishers, they must be included in marketing strategies. As seen in the two examples (Amazon Prime and 4bro), celebrities on TikTok are becoming more powerful and influential, and this will probably increase in the future.

6 Conclusion

The focus of this research was to assess how social media marketing works in the self-media era, with special focus on the video-sharing platform Tik-Tok. Existing literature has shown that marketing strategies such as influencer marketing and video marketing are becoming more popular and very powerful. In addition, the research experiment contributes to future marketing methods that brands can use for guidance in building their own TikTok channels, providing knowledge about the platform and algorithm. Furthermore, this study showed how brands can work together with influencers; the use of web celebrities for advertising purposes is becoming more popular and combining this with other marketing methods (for example, viral marketing) can create a successful campaign on TikTok. Thus, advertisers should focus more on user-generated content in the self-media era.

Moreover, TikTok and social media in general lead to narcissism and social comparison. The users who become self-publishing consumers, tend to compare themselves with others, for instance with Charli D´Amelio, and therefore the effect of social comparison has increased with the use of this platform. Charli D´Amelio´s success is hard to explain, because she presents herself as a typical normal teenage girl. But now, she acts as a role model for millions of young girls. These are all important aspects to consider when doing social media marketing on TikTok. The presentation of the self is a crucial factor in social media and should always play an important role.

The video marketing sector is becoming important for advertisement due to the fact that people can watch short videos almost anywhere on their smartphones. However, gamification and AI are also important factors in social media marketing that contribute to its addictive characteristics. TikTok focuses on improving these features to keep people using the platform for the long term. Future research can determine the progress.

These are all elements of how social media marketing works in the self-media era, and TikTok is the platform that best reflects this.

7 Study Limitations and Recommendations for Future Research

Several limitations in this study should be considered for future research. To begin, I did not work with a specific company or brand, having received no response when I contacted them. I probably have too few followers, or many of the companies may not have been interested in TikTok yet, which is likely to change in the future. I also did not have the opportunity to run ads on TikTok because I do not have a business. However, it would be interesting for future studies to analyze how TikTok ads perform in terms of clicking and buying behavior.

Another limitation was that TikTok is quite a new platform, so there is not much scientific literature about it. In addition, I started my TikTok channel in August 2020 and only conducted the experiment until the end of the year. It would be insightful to assess if the statistics change after a year of activity.

Finally, for future research, I would also recommend analyzing the algorithm and its changes in more detail.

8 Reference List

Anderson, S. L. (2017). Watching People Is Not a Game: Interactive Online Corporeality, Twitch.tv and Videogame Streams. *Game Studies*, *17*(1), 1–16.

Barry, C. T., Doucette, H., Loflin, D. C., Rivera-Hudson, N., & Herrington, L. L. (2017). "Let me take a selfie": Associations between self-photography, narcissism, and self-esteem. *Psychology of Popular Media Culture*, *6*(1), 48–60.

Bennett, W. (2020, August 27). Charli D'Amelio Is the Most Famous Person in the World — Interview. Retrieved 2.1.2021, from https://www.allure.com/story/charli-damelio-tiktok-interview

Berger, J., & Milkman, K. L. (2012). What Makes Online Content Viral? *Journal of Marketing Research*, *49*(2), 192–205.

Buffardi, L. E., & Campbell, W. K. (2008). Narcissism and Social Networking Web Sites. *Personality and Social Psychology Bulletin*, *34*(10), 1303–1314.

Carpenter, C. J. (2012). Narcissism on Facebook: Self-promotional and anti-social behavior. *Personality and Individual Differences*, *52*(4), 482–486.

Carter, D. (2016). Hustle and Brand: The Sociotechnical Shaping of Influence. *Social Media + Society*, 1–12.

Cheng, X., Liu, J., & Dale, C. (2013). Understanding the Characteristics of Internet Short Video Sharing: A YouTube-Based Measurement Study. *IEEE Transactions on Multimedia*, *15*(5), 1184–1194.

Chou, H. T., & Edge, N. (2012). 'They are happier and having better lives than I am': the impact of using Facebook on perceptions of others' lives. *Cyberpsychology, Behavior, and Social Networking*, *15*(2), 117–121.

Content Marketing Institute. (2015). *B2B CONTENT MARKETING 2015 Benchmarks, Budgets, and Trends— North America*. Retrieved 19.12.2020 https://contentmarketinginstitute.com/wp-content/uploads/2014/10/2015_B2B_Research.pdf

De Veirman, M., Hudders, L., & Nelson, M. R. (2019). What Is Influencer Marketing and How Does It Target Children? A Review and Direction for Future Research. *Frontiers in Psychology, 10*, 2685.

Dilon, C. (2020). Tiktok Influences on Teenagers and Young Adult Students: The Common Usages of The Application TikTok. *American Scientific Research Journal for Engineering, Technology, and Sciences, 68*(1), 132–142.

Elsässer, S. (2020, September 8). *Die Zielgruppe kennen*. StartupValley Magazine. Retrieved 19.12.2020 from https://www.startupvalley.news/de/4bro/

Firsching, J. (2020). *TikTok Statistiken 2020: 100 Mio. Nutzer in Europa & über 800 Mio. weltweit*. FUTUREBIZ. Retrieved 19.12.2020 from https://www.futurebiz.de/artikel/tiktok-statistiken-2019/

Frankenfield, J. (2020, March 12). *Artificial Intelligence (AI)*. Investopedia. Retrieved 19.12.2020 from https://www.investopedia.com/terms/a/artificial-intelligence-ai.asp

Gong, Y. (2019). Analysis on the 'Joint' Marketing Strategy of New Media. *Advances in Social Science, Education and Humanities Research, 375*, 374–378.

GRIN. (2020). *Influencer Discount Codes & Affiliate Links - How and when to use them in your campaigns*. GRIN - Influencer Marketing Software. Retrieved 19.12.2020 https://grin.co/blog/influencer-discount-codes-affiliate-links-how-and-when-to-use-them-in-your-campaigns/

Guinaudeau, B., Vottax, F., & Munger, K. (2020). Fifteen Seconds of Fame: TikTok and the Democratization of Mobile Video on Social Media. OSF. https://osf.io/f7ehq/download

Helm, S. (2010). Viral Marketing - Establishing Customer Relationships by 'Word-of-mouse'. *Electronic Markets, 10*(3), 158–161.

Holland, M. (2016). How YouTube Developed into a Successful Platform for User-Generated Content. *Elon Journal of Undergraduate Research in Communications, 7*(1), 1.

Hromek, R., & Roffey, S. (2009). Promoting Social and Emotional Learning With Games. *Simulation & Gaming, 40*(5), 626–644.

Reference List

Hu, Y. (2020). Research on the commercial value of TikTok in China. *Academic Journal of Business & Management*, *2*(7), 57–64.

Huotari, K., & Hamari, J. (2016). A definition for gamification: anchoring gamification in the service marketing literature. *Electronic Markets*, *27*(1), 21–31.

IGI Global. (n.d.). *What is Self-Media?* Retrieved 17.12.2020 from https://www.igi-global.com/dictionary/follow-me/77901

Influencer Marketing Hub. (2020). *What is TikTok? – The Fastest Growing Social Media App Uncovered.* Retrieved 17.12.2020 from https://influencermarketinghub.com/what-is-tiktok/

INSEAD Knowledge. (2019). *The TikTok Strategy: Using AI Platforms to Take Over the World.* Insead. Retrieved 19.12.2020 from https://faculty.insead.edu/jason-davis/documents/TikTok.pdf

Jaffar, B. A., Riaz, S., & Mushtaq, A. (2019). Living in a Moment: Impact of TikTok on Influencing Younger Generations into Micro-Fame. *Journal of Content, Community & Communication*, *10*(5), 187–194.

Johnson, M. R., & Woodcock, J. (2019). "And Today's Top Donator is": How Live Streamers on Twitch.tv Monetize and Gamify Their Broadcasts. *Social Media + Society*, 1–11.

Jung, H., & Zhou, Q. (2019). *Learning and Sharing Creative Skills with Short Videos: A Case Study of User Behavior in TikTok and Bilibili.* Retrieved 19.12.2020 from https://www.researchgate.net/publication/335335984 _Learning_and_Sharing_Creative_Skills_with_Short_Videos_A_Ca se_Study_of_User_Behavior_in_TikTok_and_Bilibili

Kennedy, M. (2020). 'If the rise of the TikTok dance and e-girl aesthetic has taught us anything, it's that teenage girls rule the internet right now': TikTok celebrity, girls and the Coronavirus crisis. *European Journal of Cultural Studies*, *23*(6), 1069–1076.

Kumar, V. D., & Prabha, M. S. (2019). Getting glued to TikTok® – Undermining the psychology behind widespread inclination toward dub-mashed videos. *Archives of Mental Health*, *20*(2), 76–77.

Lamont, T. (2020, June 6). 'It's hard to put the brakes on it. We doubled down': Charli D'Amelio and the first family of TikTok. Retrieved 2.1.2021 from https://www.theguardian.com/lifeandstyle/2020/jun/06/its-hard-to-put-the-brakes-on-it-we-doubled-down-charli-damelio-and-the-first-family-of-tiktok#

Lee, E., Lee, J.-A., Moon, J. H., & Sung, Y. (2015). Pictures Speak Louder than Words: Motivations for Using Instagram. *Cyberpsychology, Behavior, and Social Networking, 18*(9), 552–556.

Lou, C. (2020). *SPECIAL ISSUE: Future Trends in Influencer Marketing*. Nefca. Retrieved 19.12.2020 https://nefca.eu/wp-content/uploads/2020/05/Special-Issue-Influencer-Marketing.pdf

Lucassen, G., & Jansen, S. (2014). Gamification in Consumer Marketing - Future or Fallacy? *Procedia - Social and Behavioral Sciences, 148*, 194–202.

Lup, K., Rosenthal, L., & Trub, L. (2015). Instagram #instasad?: exploring associations among Instagram use, depressive symptoms, negative social comparison, and strangers followed. *Cyberpsychology, Behavior, and Social Networking, 18*(5), 247–252.

McGill, J. (2020). *How to Develop a Content Strategy: A Start-to-Finish Guide*. HubSpot. Retrieved 19.12.2020 from https://blog.hubspot.com/marketing/content-marketing-plan

Miller, A., Pater, J., & Mynatt, E. (2013). Design Strategies for Youth-Focused Pervasive Social Health Games. *2013 7th International Conference on Pervasive Computing Technologies for Healthcare and Workshops*, 9–16.

Miller, R., & Lammas, N. (2010). Social media and its implications for viral marketing. *Asia Pacific Public Relations Journal, 11*, 1–9.

Monroe, J. (2019). *Social Media Comparison & Teen Mental Health*. Newport Academy. Retrieved 19.12.2020 from https://www.newportacademy.com/resources/empowering-teens/theory-of-social-comparison/

Omar, B., & Dequan, W. (2020). Watch, Share or Create: The Influence of Personality Traits and User Motivation on TikTok Mobile Video Usage. *International Journal of Interactive Mobile Technologies (IJIM), 14*(4), 121–137.

Reference List

Ong, E. Y. L., Ang, R. P., Ho, J. C. M., Lim, J. C. Y., Goh, D. H., Lee, C. S., & Chua, A. Y. K. (2011). Narcissism, extraversion and adolescents' self-presentation on Facebook. *Personality and Individual Differences*, *50*(2), 180–185.

Peng, A., Liu, J., & Gao, Q. (2019). Public Opinion Analysis Strategy of Short Video Content Review in Big Data Environment. *2019 16th International Computer Conference on Wavelet Active Media Technology and Information Processing*, 100–104.

Rui, J., & Stefanone, M. A. (2013). Strategic self-presentation online: A cross-cultural study. *Computers in Human Behavior*, *29*(1), 110–118.

Salen, K., & Zimmerman, E. (2003). *Rules of Play: Game Design Fundamentals.* Boston: MIT Press.

Statista. (2019). *Prognose zum Marktvolumen für Influencer Marketing in der DACH-Region bis 2020*. Retrieved 19.12.2020 from https://de.statista.com/statistik/daten/studie/818786/umfrage/marktvolumen-fuer-influencer-marketing-in-der-dach-region/

Statista. (2020a). Anzahl der aktiven Social-Media-Nutzer weltweit bis 2020. Retrieved 2.1.2021 from https://de.statista.com/statistik/daten/studie/739881/umfrage/monatlich-aktive-social-media-nutzer-weltweit/

Statista. (2020b). *Downloads von TikTok über den Apple App Store in Deutschland bis November 2020*. Retrieved 19.12.2020 from https://de.statista.com/statistik/daten/studie/1028363/umfrage/anzahl-der-downloads-von-tiktok-ueber-den-apple-app-store-in-deutschland/

Statista. (2020c). *Social Networks mit den meisten Nutzern weltweit 2020*. Retrieved 19.12.2020 from https://de.statista.com/statistik/daten/studie/181086/umfrage/die-weltweit-groessten-social-networks-nach-anzahl-der-user/

The Sunday Times. (2020, May 12). TikTok: everything you need to know. Retrieved 2.1.2021 from https://www.thetimes.co.uk/article/tiktok-everything-you-need-to-know-692pnxdb2

TikTok. (n.d.). About | TikTok - Real Short Videos. Retrieved 2.1.2021 from https://www.tiktok.com/about?lang=en

TikTok (2020a). *Introducing the $200M TikTok Creator Fund*. Retrieved 19.12.2020 from https://newsroom.tiktok.com/en-us/introducing-the-200-million-tiktok-creator-fund

TikTok (2020b). *The TikTok Creator Fund is now LIVE in the UK, Germany, Italy, France and Spain, and here is how to apply!* Retrieved 19.12.2020 from https://newsroom.tiktok.com/en-gb/the-tiktok-creator-fund-is-now-live-across-europe-and-here-is-how-to-apply

Tolentino, J. (2019, September 24). How TikTok Holds Our Attention. *The New Yorker*. Retrieved 19.12.2020 from https://www.newyorker.com/magazine/2019/09/30/how-tiktok-holds-our-attention

Vargo, S. L., & Lusch, R. F. (2014). Inversions of service-dominant logic. *Marketing Theory*, *14*(3), 239–248.

Vinerean, S. (2017). Content Marketing Strategy. Definition, Objectives and Tactics. *Expert Journal of Marketing*, *5*(2), 92–98.

Wilson, R. F. (2018, May 6). *The Six Simple Principles of Viral Marketing*. Practical Ecommerce. Retrieved 19.12.2020 from https://www.practicalecommerce.com/viral-principles

Woerndl, M., Papagiannidis, S., Bourlakis, M., & Li, F. (2008). Internet-induced marketing techniques: Critical factors of viral marketing. *International Journal of Business Science and Applied Management*, *3*(1), 33–45.

Wood, J. V. (1996). What is Social Comparison and How Should We Study it? *Personality and Social Psychology Bulletin*, *22*(5), 520–537.

WordStream. (n.d.). Social Media Marketing for Businesses | WordStream. Retrieved 2 January 2021, from https://www.wordstream.com/social-media-marketing

Yang, S. (2019). *Analysis of the Reasons and Development of Short Video Application——Taking Tik Tok as an Example*. Semantic Scholar. Retrieved 19.12.2020 from https://www.semanticscholar.org/paper/Analysis-of-the-Reasons-and-Development-of-Short-as-Yang-Zhao/4e31b8d9113f1d7c5d221b63a12f7aa3d8d93518

Internet Economics / Internetökonomie
edited by / hrsg. von Prof. Dr. Julia Maintz (Cologne Business School (CBS))

Jacqueline Schmittem
Data-driven travel marketing
The importance of business intelligence for affiliate marketing in the travel industry
A dynamic business environment, various digital marketing tools and the power of data are main challenges travel companies have to face. Up-to-dateness and flexibility are crucial for increasing competitiveness and surviving in the jungle of travel firms. But how can these challenges be managed? With a holistic view, business intelligence enhances data-driven decision-making, addresses challenges and brings firms to the next level. By combining data technologies with affiliate marketing, this book develops a data-driven concept for enhanced decision-making in affiliate travel marketing.
Bd. 11, 2021, 102 S., 29,90 €, br., ISBN 978-3-643-91334-0

Athanasios Andreou
Interaktives Zusammenwirken zwischen Unternehmen, Nutzern und Online Communities: Zur Optimierung von Innovationsprozessen
Innovationen sind die Voraussetzung für den langfristigen Erfolg von Unternehmen. Jedoch erreicht eine überwältigende Mehrheit innovativer Lösungen nie die Marktreife. Als ein Hauptgrund dafür wird die fehlende Orientierung an Marktbedürfnissen angesehen. In diesem Buch werden daher Möglichkeiten aufgezeigt, wie durch die interaktive Zusammenarbeit zwischen Unternehmen, visionären Nutzern und Entwicklern von Produkten sowie Online Communities Innovationsprozesse dahingehend optimiert werden können, dass erfolgreiche Innovationen entwickelt werden.
Bd. 10, 2016, 86 S., 24,90 €, br., ISBN 978-3-643-13197-3

Mareike Müller
Online media marketing approaches of Latin American multinationals: Analyzing the integration of culture-sensitive designs
vol. 9, 2021, ca. 104 pp., ca. 34,90 €, br., ISBN-CH 978-3-643-90691-5

Mohammad-Munir Adi
The Usage of Social Media in the Arab Spring
The Potential of Media to Change Political Landscapes throughout the Middle East and Africa
The unrests, riots, revolutions and civil wars throughout the Arab Spring have undoubtedly initiated a series of chain reactions on Arab and African soil. The research analyzes the usage of the Internet and the Social Media platforms in Tunisia, Egypt and Syria in order to clarify its relevance to the uprisings.
Bd. 8, 2014, 72 S., 19,90 €, br., ISBN 978-3-643-90468-3

Laura Neises
Social CRM in the airline industry: Engaging the digital natives
Social media has found its way into most businesses as a tool to push sales. Yet its potential to create long-term customer loyalty is not fully exploited. Especially in industries characterized by fierce competition customer loyalty is key for sustainable success. But how can companies attract the future consumers? Born in the digital age, digital natives are powerful experts of social media and will dominate businesses. Building on insights from the aviation industry, this book develops an approach to use social media in a way that engages the digital natives in long-term relationships.
Bd. 7, 2013, 112 S., 17,90 €, br., ISBN 978-3-643-90397-6

Elena Trost
Social Media Marketing in BRIC Countries
Examining case studies of BMW, adidas and NIVEA
The economic growth and increasing Internet access within BRIC (Brazil, Russia, India and China) is opening new opportunities for companies to reach wider audiences.
This study examines these opportunities and assesses how global companies are capitalizing on these emerging markets; in particular the degree to which digital marketing and social CRM through social networks are being used. For the purposes of this analysis, three German brands are examined in detail: BMW, adidas and NIVEA.
The author shows that regular interaction with Internet users and monitoring of social networks can result in companies experiencing an uplift in both public perception and engagement. Another aspect addressed is the cultural variance that needs to be taken into account when planning social media activities. This study concludes that presently the full potential of social media has yet to be utilized within the BRIC countries, and that there is a unique opportunity to be realised by companies.
Bd. 6, 2013, 144 S., 19,90 €, br., ISBN 978-3-643-90264-1

Jana Louise Baum
Mobbing 2.0
Eine kultursoziologische Betrachtung des Phänomens Cyber-Mobbing
Digitale soziale Medien verändern Kommunikationsprozesse. Das Internet als neuer Raum vielfältiger Möglichkeiten bietet eine neue Freiheit, dessen größte Stärken zugleich die größten Risiken bergen. Cyber-Mobbing, ein vielschichtiges Phänomen, das viele, vor allem junge Menschen betrifft, entwickelt sich zu einem auffallend präsenten Thema unserer Gesellschaft. Der vorliegende Band analysiert nicht nur Ergebnisse soziologischer Untersuchungen zu Cyber-Mobbing, sondern liefert zudem eine Betrachtung des Themas aus medien- und kulturwissenschaftlicher Perspektive.
Bd. 5, 2015, 108 S., 19,90 €, br., ISBN 978-3-643-11809-7